The Cook Survives . . . is the ideal series of cookbooks for special occasions and particular situations. Designed by Pat McCormack to help you – the cook – enjoy yourself and keep on top of things in the kitchen, *The Cook Survives . . .* series offers useful hints for organizing your cooking, easy-to-cook tasty menus and detailed recipes packed with helpful information.

The Cook Survives . . . Bedsitland is the perfect companion for the novice and not-so-novice cook living alone.

By the same author

The Cook Survives . . . Christmas and the New Year
The Cook Survives . . . Children's Parties

PAT McCORMACK

The Cook Survives
Bedsitland

Illustrated by Geraldine Foster

GRAFTON BOOKS
A Division of the Collins Publishing Group

LONDON GLASGOW
TORONTO SYDNEY AUCKLAND

Grafton Books
A Division of the Collins Publishing Group
8 Grafton Street, London W1X 3LA

Published by Grafton Books 1986

ISBN 0-586-06641-1

Printed and bound in Great Britain by
Collins, Glasgow

Set in Bembo

Contents

Introduction

There are as many different types of 'Bedsits' as there are 'Bedsittees'. The most usual occupant is more often than not young, living away from home for the first time *and* on a limited budget. This, coupled with some most unusual cooking facilities, can make producing anything more exotic than beans on toast a nightmare!

The Cook Survives . . . Bedsitland has lots of recipes that are easy to prepare, some even on just one camping-ring! It also assumes that the reader may be unfamiliar with many cooking phrases, so is carefully compiled using the simplest of descriptions and methods that even the most

'Lots of recipes are easy to prepare even on just one camping-ring!'

spoilt 'mummy's boy' should be able to cope with! If you are already pretty 'au fait' with cookery terms and procedures, do bear with us – the ideas and recipes will still be helpful.

For many people, living in 'Bedsitland' is a time for trying out different things, so we include one or two offbeat recipes but still keep the main emphasis of the book on simply prepared, good, fresh food. Being able to cook reasonably well is smashing – it is a relaxing and rewarding hobby and once you've experienced the pleasure of serving and eating good food prepared and cooked by yourself,

'Ventilation!'

you'll be 'hooked'! It takes just as long to cook badly as to cook well, so why not start as you mean to go on. After all, if you don't think you're worth it, who will?

EQUIPMENT

The first thing to establish is whether the cooking is to be done in your room or whether there is a separate kitchen. If the answer is in the room, many points must be considered. The most important is ventilation! Unless this is excellent, forget all about chip-pans – better for your health anyway! The last thing you want to do is fill your room full of cooking smells. Air fresheners can help,

'A sharp knife is essential'

but even the strongest has problems coping with fishy-smelling curtains and upholstery! Burning eau de cologne candles is quite effective, especially with stale cigarette smoke, but again they just can't remove strong cooking smells. Of course, if money is no problem, then extractor fans and cooker-hoods are excellent and very efficient!

Electric fry-pans or multi-cookers with well-fitting lids are useful, as are the small slo-cookers and electric sandwich toasters that can convert to a grill.

A sharp knife is essential. Blunt knives are dangerous – buy a knife that feels easy in your hand and keep it sharp at all times. A Mouli-sieve is well worth considering. It can double as a colander, take lumps out of sauces or gravy, purée fruit or vegetables, and give a lovely texture to soups. It is very reasonably priced and uses no electricity!

Scales are useful but by no means essential; as a rough guide, assume that 1 rounded tablespoon = 25g (1oz). If you have no measuring jug use an empty glass milk bottle as a gauge. This same bottle will also double as a rolling pin. Pastry likes to be cold so it really is ideal for this purpose.

You will need a good strong sieve, a wooden spoon, kitchen scissors and a tin opener. A coiled wire whisk costs very little and is the best way to blend a sauce or gravy, while either a fish slice or pallet knife will save a lot of messing about when lifting small items of food from one medium to another. (Kitchen tongs are also very good for this, especially with hot meats.)

Salt and pepper mills that *work* are very desirable items since salt and pepper taste so much better freshly ground.

Do remember, though – most kitchens are over-stocked with gadgets that are seldom used. As a general rule, don't buy anything for which you have not had a use four days out of seven!

MEASURES

Both metric and imperial measures are given throughout this book; for the best results, don't mix the two up. To make life easier, wherever possible measurements are given using a spoon!

Each recipe states how many servings it supplies. While the bias of the book is towards feeding one person there are times when just one portion would be impractical, and anyway, sometimes you might want 'seconds'.

The abbreviations used in the recipes are:

g = gram(s)   in = inch(es)
ml = millilitre(s) cm = centimetre(s)
oz = ounce(s)   °C = degrees Centigrade (Celsius)
lb = pound(s)   °F = degrees Fahrenheit

INGREDIENTS

Most ingredients in this book are used fresh. Occasionally, tinned or ready-made items are called for when their taste is particularly suitable for a recipe, or time is short. Everything used is freely available. However, freshly cut herbs can make such a difference to your cooking and never seem to be in the shops when you need them. It really is a good idea to grow your own. Parsley, basil, tarragon and thyme are a good basic selection and grow happily enough in plant pots. They have the added bonus of looking attractive grouped together on a window sill and they will scent the air lightly.

Butter and olive oil are used throughout because the taste is better, but a good quality margarine or cooking oil may be substituted if wished. When shopping, don't be afraid to ask for the quantities you need, however

'Most common herbs are happy enough in plant pots and have the added bonus of looking attractive grouped together on a window sill'

small. Self-service greengrocers' are a good idea if there is one handy for you, but you will find that most good shopkeepers are happy to oblige with smaller orders, especially if they are regular!

BEFORE YOU START . . .

There are one or two instructions that appear several times in the book and so to save time and too much repetition they are explained below.

To Peel a Tomato

Put the tomato into a small heatproof container, pour over enough boiling water to cover it completely. Wait 1 minute, then plunge the tomato into cold water. The skin will now peel away easily.

To Make Fresh Breadcrumbs

Easy if you have an electric blender or coffee grinder, but if not try grating a dry piece of bread using a medium grater (it is best to remove the crusts from the bread first) or try rubbing pieces of dry bread between the palms of your hands. The bread needs to be quite dry to give satisfactory results.

To Crush a Clove of Garlic

Find a wide-bladed knife, place a garlic clove on a board and press the flat side of the blade on to the garlic sharply. The skin on the clove will split away and can be easily removed while the clove is effectively crushed.

Chopping and Slicing

Fresh herbs can be 'chopped' very well using a small pair of scissors, but when it comes to vegetables a good weighty chopping knife is best. Don't try to imitate the speed of a professional chef, but do try the technique of sliding the blade of the knife down from your knuckles. If it feels strange and cumbersome try to work out your own method. As long as the vegetables are chopped or sliced *evenly*, the way this is achieved is quite immaterial.

Soups

Making your own soup is an excellent idea. It is easily prepared, uses inexpensive ingredients and can be satisfying enough for a main meal. A pan full of soup will warm through in seconds and can keep you going through the night should you ever need to 'swot' that late, or alternatively provide a good stomach lining if you're trotting off to an 'all nighter'! With four exceptions, all of the following soups can be served straight from the pan. Ideally the carrot and coriander, leek and potato, lettuce and gazpacho need to be put through a mouli-sieve or

'Ideally the carrot and coriander, leek and potato and the two cold soups need to be put through a mouli'

blender, but with a little elbow grease and a potato masher or fork, similar textures can be achieved!

Soups follow no hard and fast rules. When making mixed vegetable soups the actual vegetables used can be whatever you have available, and the basic methods of making soup will work well using differing ingredients from the same 'family'. Parsnips or turnips, for example, could be used in place of (or as well as) carrots in the recipe for carrot and coriander soup. Dried haricot beans and a piece of neck end of lamb will make a good soup following the recipe for pea and ham, although in this case the lamb will not need to be soaked overnight.

Soups provide lots of variety, flavour and taste in return for very little effort and because of this are among the most satisfying things to make – do try!

One final point – if a mixed vegetable soup tastes as though something is missing, add a little sherry. It never fails!

The soup recipes are:

CARROT AND CORIANDER
A basic vegetable-purée soup. The coriander is a perfect complement to the sweetness of the carrots.

LEEK AND POTATO
Another vegetable-purée soup. Can be served hot or cold.

PEA AND HAM
A meat and vegetable combination soup. Very substantial, can be served as a main course.

LYONNAISE ONION SOUP
A creamy vegetable soup using the same major ingredients as the Parisienne onion soup, it is totally different in character.

PARISIENNE ONION SOUP
A browned stock vegetable soup served on a croûte base.

CHICKEN SOUP
A basic 'left-over' soup using a carcass and any vegetables you have around.

SOUPE AU PISTOU
A wonderful combination of spring vegetables, herbs and garlic. Don't be put off by the long list of ingredients, it's really simple to do and excellent when finished.

MINESTRA
An Italian vegetable combination soup – almost anything can go in this! A very close relative of minestrone.

LETTUCE SOUP
Another creamy-style vegetable soup. This recipe is most useful for using up 'tired' lettuce or outside leaves.

GAZPACHO
The classic Spanish cold 'salad' soup, marvellous on a hot day.

CARROT AND CORIANDER SOUP

Serves 2
400g (1 lb) carrots)
1 teaspoon whole coriander seeds
½ chicken stock cube } *or* substitute fresh chicken
750ml (1¼pints) water } stock
salt and freshly ground black pepper

To Cook

1) Scrape or peel the carrots (dependent on their condition) and slice into small rounds about 0.5cm (¼in) thick.
2) Put the sliced carrots into a pan with the coriander seeds, stock cube and water (or stock) and bring to the boil over a medium heat. Season very lightly with salt and pepper.
3) Turn the heat to low and simmer gently for about 30 minutes until the carrots are very soft.
4) Purée the soup by pouring into either a mouli-sieve with the finest blade fitted, or push it through a fine-mesh sieve with a wooden spoon. Discard the coriander seeds that remain in the sieve. (This soup should have a very smooth texture, so if necessary sieve twice. A liquidizer or blender can also be used but be careful not to over-do the purée when using this method.) Should the finished purée be too thick, gradually add a little more water, being careful not to 'water down' the flavour as you do so.
5) Taste for seasoning, adding salt and pepper and perhaps a little ground coriander to taste.

To Serve

Carrot and coriander soup has a lovely flavour and tastes great just as it is but for a special occasion you could stir in a dessertspoonful of cream or natural yoghurt – this will 'lift' the flavours slightly. Just stir around once when adding cream or yoghurt so that you leave a creamy trail through the orangey-coloured soup, add a sprinkling of freshly chopped parsley or watercress and 'hey, presto' a very professional finish!

LEEK AND POTATO SOUP

Serves 2–3
  200g (8oz) potatoes
  200g (8oz) leeks
  900ml (1½pints) water } *or* substitute fresh
  1 chicken stock cube   chicken stock
  salt and freshly ground black pepper

To Cook
1) Peel the potatoes. Cut into chunks about 5cm (2in) square.
2) Trim the leeks, slice into 1cm (½in) rounds and wash well to remove all grit.
3) Put the potatoes and leeks into a saucepan, add the stock cube, crumbled, then pour on the water. Season lightly with salt and pepper.
4) Bring to the boil over a medium heat, turn the heat down to low and simmer gently for 30 minutes or until the potatoes and leeks are very soft.
5) Purée the soup (*see* recipe for carrot and coriander soup, (page 20), step 4 for method).
6) Taste for seasoning, adding salt and pepper to taste.

To Serve
Leek and potato soup has several other names. It is Crème Vichysoisse when served chilled with cream swirled into

it, and Potage Parmentier when served warm. It is remarkably good either way. (If you prefer a sharper taste, use natural yoghurt as an alternative to cream.) If you like the idea of it hot but are not so sure about it cold, wait for a really hot day; the soup is especially delicious when the weather is 'too hot to eat'!

PEA AND HAM SOUP

Serves 2

1 small ham or bacon hock ⎫ soaked separately
200g (8oz) dried peas   ⎬ overnight in water
900 ml (1½pints) water (approx)
salt and freshly ground black pepper

To Cook

1) Drain the ham hock and peas and put both into a saucepan.
2) Pour over enough water to cover the hock and bring to the boil over a medium heat.
3) Skim off the froth that will appear on top of the broth. Turn the heat down to low and simmer, partially covered with a lid, for 2–3 hours until the peas are mushy and the ham is falling from the bone.
4) Add more water during the cooking period if the level of the broth falls too low. Check seasoning, adding salt and pepper to taste if needed.

To Serve

Take the ham hock from the pan and cut the meat into small dice about 1cm (½ in) square. Put these back into the soup and re-heat gently.

LYONNAISE ONION SOUP

Serves 2
    200g (8oz) onions
    25g (1oz) butter
    600ml (1pint) milk
    pinch of ground nutmeg (optional)
    salt and freshly ground black pepper

To Cook
1) Peel the onions and slice very thinly.
2) Melt the butter in a saucepan over a low heat – do not allow to brown. Add the onions and cook gently until they are soft but not brown, about 10 minutes.
3) Pour the milk over the onions, season well with salt and pepper and simmer gently for 30 minutes.
4) Taste for seasoning, adding a little ground nutmeg, if liked.

To Serve
A dessertspoonful of cream can be stirred into this soup just before serving, although the soup has quite a creamy texture without it. A tiny sprinkling of nutmeg on top of the soup looks most effective.

PARISIENNE ONION SOUP

Serves 1–2
    100g (4oz) onions
    15g (½oz) butter
    1 teaspoon flour
    600ml (1pint) good beef stock (water with 1 beef stock cube will suffice)
    1 bay leaf

salt and freshly ground black pepper
1 roll cut in half, or 2 slices of bread
a little grated cheese (Gruyère is best, but Cheddar will
  do)

To Cook
1) Peel the onions and slice them as thinly as possible.
2) Melt the butter in a saucepan, add the onion and cook
   over a low heat for 15–20 minutes, until golden-brown
   and soft.
3) Stir in the flour and cook for a further 2–3 minutes.
   Pour the stock over the onion, add the bay leaf and
   season well with salt and pepper.
4) Bring to the boil, reduce the heat and simmer for 30
   minutes. Check the seasonings and discard the bay leaf
   – if you can find it!

To Serve
Sprinkle the cheese on top of the bread and either grill or
cook in a hot oven until the cheese melts and is lightly
browned. Put the toasted bread and cheese into the bottom
of a soup bowl and ladle the hot soup over it. Serve at
once.

This is a very simple version of one of the greatest of
French soups and, although easy to make, it certainly
lacks nothing in the way of flavour.

CHICKEN SOUP (FROM LEFT-OVERS)

Serves 2–3
  1 onion
  1 leek
  1 potato
  1 small turnip

1 carrot
1 chicken carcass and giblets, but not the liver
900 ml (1½pints) water (approx)
a good pinch of thyme
1 bay leaf
3–4 sprigs of parsley
salt and freshly ground black pepper

To Cook
1) Peel the vegetables; slice the onion and leek very finely; dice the potato, turnip and carrot into 1cm (½in) squares.
2) Put the chicken carcass and giblets into a saucepan with the vegetables. Pour over the water, adding more if necessary to cover the carcass. Add the herbs and season well with salt and pepper.
3) Bring to the boil over a medium heat, skim off any froth that may appear then reduce the heat to low and simmer for 45 minutes.
4) Take out the carcass and giblets and discard. Check for seasoning.

To Serve
This soup can be served as it is from the pan or puréed (*see* carrot and coriander recipe (page 20), step 4).

The ingredients given are really intended as a guide; any vegetable could be used, although if they have been cooked already don't put them into the pan until about 10 minutes before the end of cooking time. Peas or chopped french beans are also added about 10 minutes before the soup finishes cooking and for a complete change try popping in a couple of skinned and seeded tomatoes.

SOUPE AU PISTOU

Serves 2
  50g (2oz) dried white haricot beans (soaked overnight
    in water)
  600ml (1pint) water (approx)
  100g (4oz) tomatoes ⎫
  50g (2oz) carrots
  50g (2oz) potato
  25g (1oz) leek
  25g (1oz) spring onions ⎬ approx
  25g (1oz) courgette
  25g (1oz) french beans
  2 strands of spaghetti
  1 tablespoon olive oil ⎭
  1 good pinch of saffron

For the Pistou
  1 large clove of garlic
  1 tablespoon dried basil *or*
  2 tablespoons fresh basil
  salt to taste
  1 teaspoon tomato purée
  15g (½oz) Parmesan cheese, grated
  2 tablespoons olive oil

To Cook

1) Put the soaked dried beans into a pan, cover with
   water and simmer gently for 1 hour or until the beans
   are tender. Set aside.
2) While the beans are cooking, prepare the fresh vegetables. Peel the tomatoes, (see page 13), chop the flesh
   coarsely.
3) Peel the carrots and potato and dice into 1cm (½in)

squares. Trim and wash the leek, slicing as thinly as possible.

4) Slice the spring onions, courgette and french beans thinly. Break the spaghetti into small pieces.

5) Heat the tablespoon of oil in a saucepan. Add the spring onions and cook gently until soft and just turning brown. Stir in the tomatoes and cook for one minute longer, then pour in the water and add the carrots, potato and leeks. Season well with salt and pepper.

6) Bring to the boil, then reduce the heat and simmer for 15 minutes.

7) Add the cooked haricot beans and their cooking liquid to the pan along with the french beans, courgette, spaghetti and saffron and simmer for a further 15 minutes.

8) Check for seasoning.

Pistou

While the soup is cooking, prepare the pistou. Basically what needs to be done is this: The garlic is mashed to a paste with the basil and a little salt, then extended with the tomato purée, Parmesan cheese and oil. If you have a pestle and mortar fine, otherwise improvise! A rolling pin or milk bottle rolled over the garlic a few times on a board is very effective. Once you have achieved a garlic paste, stir in the tomato purée, cheese and finally the oil.

To Serve

Ladle the hot soup into a bowl, stir the pistou into the soup to taste (usually a small teaspoonful to an average-sized bowl). (The aroma when the pistou is being stirred into the soup is marvellous and the taste – sensational!)

MINESTRA SOUP

Serves 2–3
  1 small leek
  1 small onion
  1 tomato
  1 small potato
  1 small carrot
  1 stick of celery
  4 brussels sprouts
  1 small clove garlic
  1 strand spaghetti *or* a few noodles
  1 tablespoon oil
  600ml (1pint) water
  1–2 florets of cauliflower
  1 bay leaf
  1 teaspoon freshly chopped parsley
  salt and freshly ground black pepper

To Cook
1) Trim, wash and slice the leek thinly. Peel and slice the onion. Peel the tomato and chop the flesh roughly.
2) Peel and dice the potato and carrot. Chop the celery. Halve then quarter the sprouts. Crush the garlic. Break the spaghetti into pieces.
3) Heat the oil in a saucepan over a medium heat. Add the carrot, onion and celery and cook carefully until golden. Pour the water over the vegetables, add all the other ingredients and season lightly with salt and pepper.
4) Bring to the boil, then reduce the heat and simmer for 35–40 minutes, adding more water if the soup becomes too thick.
5) Check for seasoning.

To Serve
Like most Italian soups, Minestra is particularly good
served with grated Parmesan cheese sprinkled over it.

As with the chicken soup recipe on page 24, the vegetables
used to make Minestra can be chosen from whatever you
have available – but again, if using vegetables that have
already been cooked, don't add them to the soup until 10
minutes before the end of the cooking time.

LETTUCE SOUP

Serves 1–2
    1 medium-sized lettuce *or* a few outer leaves
    1 small onion
    25g (1oz) butter
    1 teaspoon flour
    450ml (¾pint) milk
    1 teaspoon freshly chopped mint
    salt and freshly ground black pepper

To Cook
1) Wash the lettuce leaves and shred finely. Drain well.
   Peel and chop the onion into tiny dice.
2) Melt the butter over medium heat, add the lettuce and
   onion. Cover the pan, turn the heat to very low and
   cook carefully for 10 minutes. Do not allow to brown.
3) Stir in the flour and cook for 2–3 minutes longer then
   pour in the milk.
4) Simmer gently, with the pan partially covered, for 10
   minutes.
5) Purée the soup (*see* carrot and coriander recipe (page
   20) step 4). Add the chopped mint leaves. Check
   seasonings.

To Serve

For a special occasion, a little cream or natural yoghurt could be swirled into this soup, just before serving. However, it is particularly good with a few croutons tossed into it (the recipe for these appears on page 31).

GAZPACHO

Serves 2

   ½ cucumber
   ½ small onion
   1 small clove garlic
   ½ small green pepper
   2 tomatoes
   1 slice stale bread
   1 teaspoon wine vinegar
   1 tablespoon olive oil
   4 tablespoons cold water
   salt and freshly ground black pepper

To Make

1) Peel the cucumber, discard the seeds and chop the flesh roughly. Peel the onion and cut into small pieces.
2) Crush the clove of garlic, cut the pepper into small pieces, peel the tomatoes and chop the flesh roughly.
3) Remove and discard the crust from the bread and sprinkle with the vinegar.
4) Combine all the ingredients in a large bowl and set aside in a cool place for 30 minutes.
5) Purée the soup (*see* carrot and coriander recipe (page 20) step 4). Chill well for several hours. Check seasoning.

To Serve

Serve ice cold with croutons and tiny diced pieces of red or green peppers, tomatoes or cucumber. This soup has a lovely fresh taste and makes an ideal starter for a meal after a hot summer's day.

CROUTONS

Serves 4
2–3 rounds of stale bread
oil and butter – see method below

To Cook
1) Remove the crusts from the bread and discard. Cut the bread into neat dice 2 cm (¾in) square.
2) Melt the butter in the oil in a frying pan. The oil needs to be deep enough to cover a single layer of croutons. When the fat is hot, quickly fry the croutons until brown on all sides.
3) Drain on kitchen paper.

To Serve

The croutons can be made in advance and then re-heated in a hot oven for 1–2 minutes when required.

Egg Dishes

The first recipe in this section takes care of the 'Can't even boil an egg' problem and then we quickly move on to far more interesting ways to serve them! Eggs are firm favourites in all European cuisines and our recipes reflect this, from the wonderful peasanty taste of the French Piperade or Spanish Huevos à la Flamenca, to the elegant flaky pastry Brunch Mille Feuilles.

'Can't even boil an egg?'

Most egg dishes are quickly prepared, which is a decided plus when time is at a premium. The other big plus of course is the price compared to other sources of protein.

There is one rule that always applies when using eggs, and that is never use them straight from the refrigerator; they must be at room temperature. If your kitchen area is cool it may be best to buy eggs a few at a time and store them on a pretty rack, only using the fridge, if you have one, in the hottest weather.

The recipes in this section are:

How to soft boil an egg.
How to hard boil an egg.

OMELETTE
The simplest, classic and best way to make omelettes with suggestions for suitable fillings.

PANCAKES
Sweet or savoury – these are far too good to leave until Shrove Tuesday.

TORTILLA
A Spanish potato and onion 'set' omelette which can be served hot or cold.

HUEVOS A LA FLAMENCA
Another Spanish dish, this time incorporating a mixture of vegetables with baked eggs.

BRUNCH MILLE FEUILLES
Using frozen puff pastry this is a very quick and stylish way of serving bacon and eggs!

PIPERADE
The great southern French dish of scrambled eggs, smoked ham, peppers and tomatoes, it has a most memorable taste.

HOW TO SOFT BOIL AN EGG

To Cook
1) Bring a saucepan of water to the boil, reduce the heat to medium so that the water is just simmering (over-boiling water will make the whites tough).
2) Gently lower the eggs into the water and time them precisely from this moment. Follow this time chart for perfect soft-boiled eggs:
   EEC size 1 or 2   –   4 minutes
   EEC size 3 or 4   –   3½ minutes
   EEC size 5 or 6   –   3 minutes
3) As soon as the cooking time is up, take the eggs from the pan and open at once since they continue to cook from the heat generated inside the shell.

To Serve
Most of the time a sprinkling of salt and pepper and fingers of bread or toast to 'dunk' in the yolk are all that's needed to enjoy a soft-boiled egg. An interesting alternative is to pop a small knob of butter mixed with a few herbs on top of the egg, when opened, but nowadays this will probably be thought to be over-doing the fat content of the dish – tastes good though!

HOW TO HARD BOIL AN EGG

To Cook
1) Put the eggs carefully into a saucepan of cold water.
2) Bring to a simmer over medium heat (heavy boiling will make the whites leathery).
3) Time the eggs from the moment the water starts to bubble, making sure that a gentle simmer is maintained

throughout the cooking time. The times for hard-boiled eggs are:

EEC size 1 or 2   –   10 minutes
EEC size 3 or 4   –   9 minutes .
EEC size 5 or 6   –   8 minutes

4) After the correct time has elapsed take the eggs from the pan and plunge them into cold water until cooled.

5) Crack the eggs gently and peel away the thin membrane and shell together. Rinse any bits of shell away with water. If the eggs are not going to be used straight away, store them in a bowl of cold water to prevent them drying out.

To Serve

The hard-boiled eggs can be halved then quartered, or sliced, and used in salads. Alternatively cover the eggs lightly with mayonnaise or stuff them and use as a starter or even as the basis of a light meal.

To stuff a hard-boiled egg, cut it in half lengthways and gently scoop out the yolk. Push the yolk through a sieve or mash with a fork, then add a little softened butter, some freshly chopped herbs or anything else that takes your fancy – cream cheese, prawns, tuna, cod roes or small diced vegetables with a little mayonnaise to bind them, are all good. The egg can be re-formed filled with stuffing; put a small amount of filling on the serving plate and set the egg on this to stop it sliding about.

Depending on your chosen filling, serve with mayonnaise or French dressing.

OMELETTE

Serves 1
  2–3 eggs
  salt and freshly ground black pepper
  15g (½oz) butter

To Cook

1) Crack the eggs into a bowl, season lightly with salt and pepper and beat quickly with a fork just until the yolks and whites are combined.
2) Heat the butter over medium heat in a frying pan approx. 20cm (8in) in diameter. When the butter starts to foam pour in the eggs.
3) Stir the eggs around then gently draw in the setting mixture from the edges of the pan so that the remaining liquid runs underneath. The total cooking time should be only about 1 minute.
4) When the eggs are set on the bottom but still runny on top, roll the omelette over and tip on to a warmed plate.

To Serve

Omelettes must always be served immediately; they do not keep well. There are lots of different fillings to choose from. If using fresh herbs put them into the egg mixture before cooking. Grated cheese is best sprinkled on to the soft side of the omelette before rolling since it could cause the eggs to stick if added to the mixture. A little diced ham mixed with cheese gives a very substantial omelette. Other fillings could include mushrooms, pilchards, crisp bacon and mixed vegetables – the choice is yours!

PANCAKES

Makes 2–4 pancakes
  1 egg
  pinch of salt
  50g (2oz) plain flour
  75ml (⅛pint) milk
  1 tablespoon water
  15g (½oz) melted butter
  15g (½oz) butter ⎱
  1 teaspoon oil ⎰ to cook the pancakes

To Cook

1) Stir the egg, salt and flour together in a bowl. Gradually add the milk and water and beat well with a wire whisk. Stir in the melted butter and beat well again.
2) Allow the batter to rest in a cool place for at least 30 minutes before using.
3) Melt the butter in the oil. Set aside.
4) Using a small frying pan over medium heat, smear a little of the butter/oil mixture over the base of the pan. When hot pour in a small amount of batter (2 tablespoons should be ample) and tip the pan around so that the batter runs over the base of the pan (the pancakes must be as thin as possible).
5) As soon as the mixture sets (after 30–40 seconds), flip the pancake over with a spatula (or toss it with a splendiferous wrist action) and cook the underside for 20–30 seconds. Slide the pancake on to a warmed plate.

To Serve

Pancakes can be cooked ahead of time and kept covered until needed. To re-heat, cover in foil and pop into a hot oven for 5 minutes or so. Prise them apart gently.

If the pancakes are for dessert, serve them with jam, lemon juice and sugar, fresh fruits, ice cream, melted chocolate and nuts – whatever is your favourite. If they are to be savoury, then a little more work is needed. Savoury fillings for pancakes are best held together with a white sauce and by far the easiest way of making that is as follows:

15g (½oz) butter
150ml (¼pint) milk
15g (½oz) flour
pinch of salt

Put all these ingredients cold into a pan. Set over medium heat and stir with a wooden spoon, whisk or fork until blended then simmer gently for 3–4 minutes. To finish add whatever you fancy, say seafood, ham and chopped walnuts, mushrooms, cheese and cooked broccoli, diced sautéed chicken livers – whatever you have available, don't be afraid to experiment! Just pop a spoonful of filling in the centre of each pancake and roll up!

TORTILLA

Serves 1
1 medium-sized potato
1 small onion
a little butter and oil
2–3 eggs
salt and freshly ground black pepper

To Cook
1) Peel the potato and slice thinly, say 0.5cm (¼in) thick. Peel and slice the onion as thinly as you can.
2) Heat a knob of butter with a tablespoonful of oil over medium heat in a frying pan. Add the potato and

onion slices and cook steadily until well browned and cooked through.

3) Break the eggs into a bowl, season lightly with salt and pepper and beat well. Gently stir in the potato and onion.

4) Melt a little more butter in oil in a medium-sized frying pan. When the foam subsides pour in the egg mixture.

5) Gently draw the mixture across the pan once or twice, then turn the heat to low and cook gently until the top is just about to set.

6) Cover the pan with a large flat plate, invert, then carefully slide the tortilla back into the pan and cook the underside for 1–2 minutes.

To Serve

Tortilla can be eaten hot or cold. If serving it hot, crispy smoked bacon or Spanish chorizo sausages are good accompaniments. When served cold it can be used as a tasty addition to a cold buffet table and makes an interesting change from cold quiche.

HUEVOS A LA FLAMENCA

Serves 1–2

½ small clove garlic
1 small onion
½ small green pepper
½ small red pepper
1 large tomato
1 chorizo sausage (optional)
15g (½oz) butter
1 teaspoon olive oil
1 tablespoon peas cooked or frozen
1 teaspoon freshly chopped parsley

salt and freshly ground black pepper
2 eggs
1 teaspoon dry sherry

To Cook

1) Chop the garlic finely. Peel and chop the onion into tiny dice. De-seed and chop the peppers into small strips.
2) Peel the tomato, discard the seeds and chop the flesh roughly. Slice the sausage into thin rounds.
3) Melt the butter in the oil in a frying pan over medium heat. Cook the onion, garlic and pepper strips until soft but not brown.
4) Add the tomato, peas, parsley and sausage, season lightly and cook for 2–3 minutes.
5) Make 2 'wells' in the mixture and break an egg into each. Sprinkle the whole dish with sherry, cover with a lid or foil and cook over a low heat until the egg whites are set. The yolks should be 'runny'.

To Serve

Use a fish slice, if available, to lift the eggs from the pan on to the serving dish, arrange the vegetables around, sprinkle with a little more chopped parsley and serve at once.

BRUNCH MILLE FEUILLES

Serves 2

200g (8oz) puff pastry, frozen but de-frosted
2 rashers bacon
2–3 eggs
salt and freshly ground black pepper
25g (1oz) butter
1 tablespoon milk

To Cook

1) Preheat the oven to 200°C (400°F) Gas Mark 7.
2) Divide the pastry into two portions and roll out on a lightly floured board into two rectangles measuring about 20 × 10cm (8 × 4in). Place on a greased baking sheet and cook in the preheated oven for 10–12 minutes until risen and golden brown.
3) While the pastry cooks, make the filling. First grill the bacon until crisp and snip into small pieces.
4) Beat the eggs lightly, season well with salt and pepper.
5) Melt the butter in the milk in a small pan over medium heat. Pour in the egg mixture and scramble with a fork until soft curds form (the mixture needs to be quite sloppy). Remove from the heat and stir in the bacon snippets.
6) Spread the egg and bacon mixture over one piece of pastry and place the remaining pastry portion on top. Press down lightly.

To Serve

Cut into slices through the layers of pastry and serve right away. A tomato garnish looks pretty with the mille feuilles and the sharpness gives a good contrast of flavours.

PIPERADE

Serves 1–2

> 1 spring onion
> ½ small clove garlic
> ½ small green pepper
> 2 tomatoes
> ½ slice smoked ham, cooked
> 2 teaspoons olive oil
> a good pinch of fresh or dried basil

salt and freshly ground black pepper
1 teaspoon freshly chopped parsley
15g (½oz) butter
2–3 eggs

To Cook

1) Chop the onion, garlic and green pepper finely.
2) Peel the tomatoes, discard the seeds and chop the flesh roughly. See page 13.
3) Cut the ham into small strips.
4) Heat 1 teaspoon of olive oil in a small pan. Add the onion, garlic and peppers and cook until soft but not browned.
5) Add the tomatoes, basil, salt and pepper and cook slowly until the tomatoes turn to a pulp, adding a little water if the mixture looks too dry. Stir in the parsley.
6) Break the eggs into a bowl, season lightly and beat until the yolks and whites combine.
7) Melt the butter in the remaining oil in a saucepan. Pour in the eggs and scramble until they form soft curds. Remove from the heat and turn the eggs onto a warmed plate.

To Serve

Spread the tomato mixture over the eggs, cutting into them so that the two combine. Scatter the pieces of ham on top and serve straight away.

Meat and Poultry

Do try to find a good butcher; sometimes a few pence more per kilo is well worth it, and less fat to trim away means fewer pennies chucked into the dustbin! For some reason young men shopping for meat seem particularly vulnerable. I remember a while ago being told of a 'most helpful, jolly butcher' who insisted on 'looking after' four lads sharing a flat nearby. Every Saturday, he gathered together a carrier-bag full of bits of meat, bones, gristle

'Make up kebabs by sliding pieces of
vegetable or fruit between cubes of meat
onto a skewer'

and all, and saved it for them. No matter what they asked for, the bag was what they got and invariably its contents ended up in the bin!

The recipes included in this section are mainly casseroles or 'made-up' dishes and grills. Sadly, roasting in small quantities is just too impractical given the cost of a decent-sized joint of meat these days. However, the following dishes are all so tasty that the exclusion of this one method of cooking shouldn't matter one bit!

There is only one problem when it comes to grilling meat – you just have to use the very best quality cuts. One way of using less meat is to make up kebabs by sliding pieces of vegetable or fruit between cubes of meat onto a skewer. The result is surprisingly more filling than the same amount of meat left in one piece. There are recipes for four different kebabs but this is yet another area of cooking where experimenting a little is much more fun!

The recipes in this section are:

GAMMON WITH SLICED APPLE AND CHEESE
A really delicious alternative to the more common pineapple garnish which will appeal to those with more savoury tastes.

CARPET BAG STEAK
Not, alas, with oysters, this version has a ham and mushroom stuffing and is lovely for a very special occasion.

LAMB CUTLET WITH A MINT CRUST
A very easy way to make a lamb chop fit for a king! The meat is best prepared up to 24 hours before cooking so that the flavours develop.

DEVILLED CHICKEN LEGS

A most useful recipe, the chicken drumsticks cooked in this way are equally good cold and are especially popular at parties.

HOME-MADE BEEF BURGERS WITH A FRESH TOMATO SAUCE

Nothing like the ready-made beef burgers, these are extra special and good enough to serve at a dinner party – well, an informal one anyway! The secret is in the technique; the meat is chopped rather than minced.

KEBABS – TERIAKI STEAK
BACON AND PEPPERS
LIVER AND KIDNEY
LAMB AND COURGETTE

It couldn't be easier to make a kebab. Two of our recipes have a marinade to flavour and tenderize the meat before cooking. The skewers can be assembled earlier in the day and cooked just when needed.

CHILLI CON CARNE

A simple made-up meal. No apologies for the use of tinned tomatoes or ready-cooked beans, either, since they give just the right combination of flavours.

LIVER AND BACON WITH TOMATOES

A good casserole which can be cooked on top of the stove or in the oven. It has a lovely flavour because the tomatoes combine so well with liver and bacon.

LANCASHIRE HOT POT

The simplest version, and without doubt the best, of this northern dish. This is how they make it in East Lancashire,

Ramsbottom to be precise. Red cabbage is a must to serve with it.

BEEF STEW WITH DUMPLINGS
The best stew around, it cooks on top of the stove, smells great and served with its own dumplings needs no other vegetables.

SPAGHETTI BOLOGNESE
Another classic that everyone has a different recipe for. This one is simple and tastes good, what more can one ask!

SHEPHERD'S PIE
A slightly different recipe in that the potatoes are sliced and crispy rather than mashed. A good dish especially in winter.

LAMB WITH YOGHURT AND CORIANDER
A dish with a Middle-Eastern feel, not hot – it has a mellow spicey taste and is very smooth.

PORK SPARE RIBS WITH SAUERKRAUT
Cooked in lager, which goes so well both with the pork and the sauerkraut, this is another dish where no other vegetables are needed.

CHICKEN CASSEROLE
A simple casserole flavoured with tomatoes; again the tinned ones are best for this dish. A mixture of mustard, Worcestershire sauce and lemon juice give a lightly spiced taste which adds interest.

GAMMON WITH SLICED APPLE AND CHEESE

Serves 1

    1 slice of gammon about 1.5cm (½in) thick
    1 small hard green eating apple
    50g (2oz) cheese, sliced wafer thin

To Cook

1) Pre-heat the grill for 2–3 minutes. Derind the gammon, snipping the fat edge to make sure it lies flat when cooked. Grill on one side for about 5 minutes until just cooked through.
2) Core the apple but leave on the skin. Cut into very thin rounds.
3) When the gammon has cooked on one side, turn it over and arrange the apple slices on top of it, cover with the sliced cheese and return to the grill.
4) Grill until the cheese is bubbling and lightly browned.

To Serve

Turn on to a warmed plate and serve with a fresh green vegetable and perhaps a few sautéed potatoes.

CARPET BAG STEAK

Serves 1

    1 tablespoon mushrooms
    1 tablespoon cooked ham
    15g (½oz) butter
    salt and freshly ground black pepper
    1 teaspoon mushroom ketchup *or* Worcestershire sauce
      (optional)

1 steak cut 2cm (¾in) thick (sirloin, rump or fillet can
    be used)
a little melted butter

To Cook
1) Pre-heat the grill. Wipe the mushrooms and chop into
    tiny dice. Snip the ham into small pieces. Mix the
    chopped mushrooms and ham together with the butter
    and season well. Add the sauce, if using.
2) Cut a slit through the centre of the steak lengthways
    leaving one side intact – the idea is to make a pocket.
3) Push the ham mixture into the pocket and secure with
    a cocktail stick. Brush the meat with melted butter and
    grill for about 5 minutes per side for a medium steak.

To Serve
Take out the cocktail stick and serve the steak cut in slices
down through the meat and stuffing.

LAMB CUTLET WITH A MINT CRUST

Serves 1
3 tablespoons breadcrumbs
1 teaspoon mint sauce
¼ clove garlic, crushed
pinch of sugar
salt and freshly ground black pepper
1–2 lamb cutlets

To Cook
1) Firstly make the breadcrumbs (*see* 'Before you start'
    page 13).
2) Mix the breadcrumbs, mint sauce, garlic, sugar and
    some salt and pepper together in a small bowl then

spread this mixture evenly over both sides of each chop. If possible allow the chops to stand in a cool place for several hours.

3) Pre-heat the grill then cook the chops for about 5 minutes each side until the topping is well-browned and crisp and the meat is just pink on the bone.

To Serve

Put the chops on to a warmed plate, decorate with cutlet frills and serve with a twist of lemon.

DEVILLED CHICKEN LEGS

Serves 1

2–3 chicken drumsticks
½ small carrot ⎫
½ small onion ⎬ roughly chopped
1 stick of celery ⎭
salt and freshly ground black pepper
25g (1oz) butter
1 tablespoon mango chutney
1 tablespoon Worcestershire sauce
1 tablespoon tomato ketchup
a dash of tabasco sauce

To Cook

1) Put the chicken legs into a small saucepan with the carrot, onion and celery. Cover with cold water, season and bring to the boil.

2) Turn the heat to low and simmer for 10 minutes.

3) While the chicken cooks, make the devilled mixture by creaming the butter then mashing into it the chutney and sauces.

4) Drain the chicken legs (reserve the stock for another recipe) and set aside to cool.
5) Skin the chicken legs and cover with the devilled mixture. (At this point the chicken can be set aside until needed.)
6) Pre-heat the grill; cook the drumsticks, basting with the devilled sauce, for 5–6 minutes turning once or twice as they cook.

To Serve
Equally good hot or cold, these chicken drumsticks could be served with a salad or with warm vegetables. They are quite sticky though, so cutlet frills or paper napkins will be needed.

HOME-MADE BEEF BURGERS WITH A FRESH TOMATO SAUCE

Serves 1
150g (6oz) lean steak, sirloin or rump
1 teaspoon very finely chopped onion (optional)
salt and freshly ground black pepper
1 small onion
½ small green pepper
½ small clove garlic
2 tomatoes
25g (1oz) butter
1 tablespoon olive oil
¼ teaspoon oregano or marjoram

To Cook
1) Make up the burgers first so that they stand and 'rest' for a minute or two whilst you make the sauce.
2) Using your sharpest knife, trim the steak of all fat,

then cut the meat into rough cubes. Spread these out into a single layer then start to chop using a flowing and rhythmic action and scraping the meat back into the middle as it spreads out. (Music might help to get the right sort of arm action.) It is important to chop the meat rather than mash it, so do make sure that the knife *is* sharp and do take lots of time to ensure the meat is finely and evenly chopped.

3) Season the chopped meat and add the chopped onion. Form the mixture into two neat rounds and flatten slightly – the burgers are best about 2cm (¾in) thick. Set aside.

4) To make the sauce, first peel and chop the onion finely, de-seed and chop the pepper, crush the garlic.

5) Peel the tomatoes, discard the seeds and chop the flesh roughly.

6) Melt 15g (½oz) butter in half the oil and cook the onion, garlic and pepper until soft but not brown.

7) Add the tomatoes and oregano and season lightly with salt and pepper. Cook for 4–5 minutes until the tomato has become a pulp, adding a little water if the sauce appears to be getting too dry. Keep warm.

8) Melt the remaining butter and oil in a small frying pan; when hot put in the burgers and cook for 3 minutes each side for rare or 4 minutes each side for medium.

To Serve

If you want to serve these burgers in a sesame seed bun that's fine, otherwise serve them with a salad or some good fresh vegetables, lightly cooked, and hand the sauce separately.

TERIAKI STEAK KEBAB

Serves 1
    150g (6oz) steak, sirloin or rump
    1 tablespoon soy sauce
    1 tablespoon dry sherry *or* sake
    ¼ clove garlic, crushed
    ¼ teaspoon ground ginger
    ¼ teaspoon sugar
    1 small onion
    2 button mushrooms
    1 small tomato

To Cook

1) Trim the meat of fat and cut into cubes 2.5cm (1in) thick.
2) Make the marinade by combining the soy sauce and sherry (or sake) and then add the crushed garlic, ginger and sugar.
3) Stir the cubes of meat into the marinade and leave in a cool place for at least 1 hour.
4) Peel and halve the onion lengthways. Wipe the mushrooms and tomato. Thread the vegetables on to a skewer between cubes of the marinated meat.
5) Pre-heat the grill then cook the kebab for 5–6 minutes, turning once or twice.

To Serve

Slide the meat and vegetables from the skewer on to a bed of plain boiled rice.

BACON AND PEPPER KEBAB

Serves 1
   2 rashers of bacon
   1 small green pepper
   1 small onion
   1 small tomato

To Cook

1) De-rind the bacon and cut each rasher in half, roll up loosely. De-seed and cut the pepper into pieces about 2cm (¾in) square. Peel the onion and cut in half lengthways. Wipe the tomato.
2) Thread the bacon and vegetables alternately on to a skewer.
3) Pre-heat the grill and cook the kebab for 5–8 minutes, turning once or twice, until the bacon is crisp and lightly browned.

To Serve

Slide the bacon and vegetables from the skewer on to a bed of savoury rice.

LIVER AND KIDNEY KEBAB

Serves 1
   2 lamb's kidneys
   100g (4oz) lamb's liver
   1 rasher of bacon
   salt and freshly ground black pepper
   a little olive oil

To Cook

1) Split the kidneys lengthways, removing the fine skin

as you do so. De-rind the bacon and cut the rasher in
two. Cut the liver into 2.5cm (1in) squares.
2) Thread the meats alternately on to a skewer. Season
well and brush with oil.
3) Pre-heat the grill and cook the kebab for 5–6 minutes,
until the bacon is crisp and the liver and kidney are still
just pink in the middle.

To Serve

Slide the meats from the skewer on to a warmed serving
plate and sprinkle with a little freshly chopped parsley. A
lightly spiced rice goes well with this kebab.

LAMB AND COURGETTE KEBAB

Serves 1

150g (6oz) lean boned lamb, cut from the shoulder or
    leg
2 tablespoons natural yoghurt
¼ small clove garlic, crushed
good pinch of ground cumin
good pinch of ground coriander
¼ teaspoon ground ginger
salt and freshly ground black pepper
1 medium-sized courgette

To Cook

1) Trim the meat of any fat and cut into 2.5cm (1in)
cubes.
2) Mix together the yoghurt, garlic and spices. Season
lightly. Stir in the cubes of lamb and set aside for at
least 30 minutes.
3) Trim the courgette and slice into 1cm (⅜in) rounds.
Bring a small saucepan of lightly salted water to the

boil, put in the courgette pieces and simmer for 1 minute only; drain well.
4) Thread the lamb on to a skewer interspaced with the courgette slices.
5) Pre-heat the grill and cook the kebab, turning once or twice, for 8–10 minutes until the lamb is browned on the outside but still just pink inside.

To Serve
Slide the lamb and courgettes from the skewer on to a warmed serving plate. Serve with a twist of lemon and crisp new potatoes.

CHILLI CON CARNE

Serves 1–2
  1 medium onion
  1 tablespoon olive oil
  150g (6oz) lean minced beef
  ½ teaspoon hot chilli powder
  1 × 425g (15oz) cooked red kidney beans
  1 small tin tomatoes
  salt

To Cook
1) Peel and chop the onion. Heat the oil in a medium-sized saucepan, add the onion and cook until soft and golden brown.
2) Put the mince into the pan and brown well. Add the chilli powder.
3) Drain the kidney beans but leave the tomatoes in their juice and add both to the pan. Season with a little salt and cook over a low heat for 30 minutes, until the mince is tender.

To Serve
Serve straight from the cooking pot with jacket potatoes
or crisp French bread.

LIVER AND BACON WITH TOMATOES

Serves 1–2
 150g (6oz) pig's liver
 1 small onion
 2 rashers bacon
 1 tablespoon olive oil
 1 small tin tomatoes
 ¼ teaspoon oregano or marjoram
 ½ teaspoon Worcestershire sauce
 salt and freshly ground black pepper

To Cook
1) Slice the liver into 1cm (⅜in) thick pieces. Peel and
 slice the onion. De-rind and cut the bacon into small
 pieces.
2) Heat the oil and cook the onion until soft and golden
 brown. Drain and set aside.
3) Cook the bacon pieces in their own fat until well
 browned. Add the sliced liver and brown on both
 sides.
4) Stir in the tomatoes and onion, add the oregano (or
 marjoram) and Worcestershire sauce; season with salt
 and pepper. Cover and cook gently on top of the stove
 for 30–35 minutes. Alternatively, put into an oven-
 proof dish and cook at 180°C (350°F) Gas Mark 4 for
 about 40 minutes.

To Serve
Skim any fat from the top of the casserole either by

blotting with kitchen paper or pieces of dried bread. Serve straight from the cooking pot, sprinkled with a little freshly chopped parsley.

LANCASHIRE HOT POT

Serves 1–2
   400g (1lb) potatoes
   200g (8oz) onions
   2 lamb chops, best end of neck or loin
   salt and freshly ground black pepper
   300ml (½pint) beef stock (made from a stock cube)

To Cook
1) Peel and slice the potatoes and onions thinly.
2) Trim the fat from the lamb.
3) Arrange the potatoes and onions in layers in a small oven-proof casserole dish. Season lightly between the layers. Pour over the stock, adding a little more water if necessary to cover the vegetables.
4) Put the chops on top of the potatoes and onions, cover tightly and cook at 180°C (350°F) Gas Mark 4 for 1½ hours, until the chops are browned and the potatoes cooked through.

To Serve
Serve straight from the cooking pot with a generous helping of red cabbage.

BEEF STEW WITH DUMPLINGS

Serves 1–2
   150g (6oz) chuck or shoulder steak

25g (1oz) plain flour
1 large onion
1 medium-sized carrot
15g (½oz) dripping or butter
300ml (½pint) beef stock (made from a stock cube)
salt and freshly ground black pepper
50g (2oz) self-raising flour
25g (1oz) shredded suet
½ teaspoon mixed herbs

To Cook

1) Trim the meat of fat and cut into cubes 2.5cm (1in) square. Toss them in the plain flour and coat well. Peel and slice the onion. Scrape and chop the carrot into small dice.
2) Heat the dripping (or butter) in a medium-sized pan; when hot brown the pieces of meat a few at a time, putting each batch on to a plate when browned.
3) When all the meat is browned put it back into the pan with the onion and carrot. Pour over the stock and season lightly. Cover the pan tightly with a lid and cook over a very low heat for 1¼–1½ hours, or until the meat is very tender.
4) While the meat is cooking, prepare the dumplings. Mix the self-raising flour and suet together in a small bowl, add a pinch of salt, the mixed herbs and just enough cold water to bind the mixture together.
5) Using your hands, dipped in flour, form 2–3 dumplings and set aside to rest for 30 minutes.
6) Twenty minutes before the end of the cooking time, put the dumplings into the top of the stew and let them simmer gently until the meat is cooked.

To Serve

Lift the dumplings out of the pan with a slotted spoon.

Sprinkle the stew with freshly chopped parsley and serve around the dumplings on a warmed plate.

SPAGHETTI BOLOGNESE

Serves 1
1 small onion
1 stick of celery
1 small carrot
½ small clove garlic
15g (½oz) butter
1 teaspoon olive oil
150g (6oz) lean minced beef
1 small tin tomatoes
½ beef stock cube
4 black peppercorns
¼ teaspoon marjoram
1 bay leaf
½ teaspoon tomato purée
salt and freshly ground black pepper
as much long spaghetti as desired
grated Parmesan cheese (optional)

To Cook
1) Peel and chop the onion finely, cut the celery and carrot into small dice. Crush the garlic.
2) Heat the butter and oil together in a medium-sized saucepan and cook the onion, celery, garlic and carrot until lightly browned. Add the peppercorns.
3) Add the meat to the pan and brown well, then pour over the tomatoes in their juice, crumble in the stock cube, add the herbs and tomato purée and season well. Add a little water if the mixture looks dry.

4) Simmer slowly for 30–40 minutes, until the mince is tender. Check the seasoning.
5) Bring a large pan of lightly salted water to the boil and gently push in the spaghetti which will soften and curl around the pan as you push it. Boil lightly for 10 minutes then drain well.

To Serve
Arrange the drained spaghetti on a warmed plate, pile the sauce on top then sprinkle with grated Parmesan cheese.

SHEPHERD'S PIE

Serves 1–2
  400g (1lb) potatoes
  1 small onion
  50g (2oz) button mushrooms
  25g (1oz) butter or dripping
  200g (8oz) lean minced beef
  150ml (¼pint) beef stock (made from a stock cube)
  salt and freshly ground black pepper

To Cook
1) Peel the potatoes and slice thinly, about 0.5cm (¼in) thick. Bring to the boil in lightly salted water. Drain immediately and set aside.
2) Peel and slice the onion. Wipe and slice the mushrooms.
3) Melt half the butter (or dripping) in a frying pan and cook the onion until soft and brown.
4) Add the mince to the pan and brown well. Stir in the mushrooms and cook for 1 minute longer. Pour over the stock, season well and mix gently. Cook for 10–15 minutes.
5) Put the meat mixture into an oven-proof dish, arrange

the potatoes over the top and dot with the remaining butter. Cook in the oven at 180°C (350°F) Gas Mark 4 for 30 minutes or until the potatoes are golden brown and crisp.

To Serve
Serve straight from the cooking pot with a good crunchy green vegetable.

LAMB WITH YOGHURT AND CORIANDER

Serves 1–2
 200g (8oz) lean boned lamb cut from the shoulder or leg
 2 tablespoons olive oil
 1 small onion
 ½ small clove garlic
 ¼ teaspoon fresh ginger root, peeled and grated, *or* ground ginger
 15g (½oz) slivered almonds
 ¼ teaspoon ground cumin
 ¼ teaspoon ground coriander
 5 tablespoons natural yoghurt
 salt and cayenne pepper

To Cook
1) Trim and discard any fat from the meat and cut into cubes about 2.5cm (1in) thick. Heat the oil in a medium-sized pan and brown the meat, a few pieces at a time, setting the meat on one side once browned.
2) Peel and slice the onion and cook in the remaining hot oil with the garlic and ginger until soft and browned.
3) Add the almonds and spices and cook for a further 2 minutes then return the cubes of meat to the pan, pour

over the yoghurt, season with a little salt and cayenne pepper and cook over a low heat for 1 hour until the meat is very tender.

To Serve

Serve with plain boiled rice and a sweet spicy chutney (such as mango).

PORK SPARE RIBS WITH SAUERKRAUT

Serves 1

   1 teaspoon olive oil
   1–2 pork spare rib chops
   1 small tin sauerkraut
   1 teaspoon soft brown sugar
   3–4 tablespoons lager
   salt and freshly ground black pepper

To Cook

1) Heat the oil in a medium-sized saucepan. Add the spare rib chops and brown on both sides.
2) Stir in the sauerkraut, sugar and enough lager to cover the two, then season well with salt and pepper.
3) Cover tightly with a lid and cook over a very low heat for 1 hour turning the chops once, until they are very tender. This dish can also be cooked in the oven at 180°C (350°F) Gas Mark 4, for 1–1½ hours.

To Serve

Serve straight from the cooking pot, perhaps with potatoes and sprinkled with freshly chopped parsley.

CHICKEN CASSEROLE

Serves 1
  15g (½oz) butter
  1 chicken portion
  1 small onion
  1 small tin tomatoes
  ¼ teaspoon French mustard
  a good dash Worcestershire sauce
  1 teaspoon soft brown sugar
  1 teaspoon lemon juice
  salt and freshly ground black pepper

To Cook
1) Melt the butter in a small frying pan. Skin the chicken then brown in the hot fat on all sides. Put the chicken into a small oven-proof dish.
2) Peel and slice the onion. Cook in the remaining hot fat until soft and lightly browned. Stir in the tomatoes, mustard, sauce, sugar and lemon juice. Season well and bring to the boil. Pour over the chicken and cover with a lid.
3) Cook the casserole in a medium oven at 180°C (350°F) Gas Mark 4 for ½ hour or until the chicken is tender. Check the seasoning.

To Serve
Skim any fat from the top of the casserole by blotting with kitchen paper or pieces of dry bread. Sprinkle with some freshly chopped parsley and serve straight from the casserole dish.

Fish

Fish is such a delicious source of all that's good for you that it would be a pity to miss out because of the smell! To minimize any unpleasant aromas wafting about your room, the following recipes have been chosen because they are either cooked covered or so quickly it will hardly matter.

Fish is very easy to cook and you will find that the same basic methods will apply to most varieties. River trout will bake in the same way as sea bass or red mullet; plaice can almost always be substituted for sole and cod; monk fish steaks can take the place of the more expensive halibut or salmon. Although the flavours are different the same sauces or butters will complement the different fishes just as well.

A good fresh fish is always better than a frozen one and your fishmonger will clean the fish for you; all that remains is to cook it!

The recipes in this section are:

COD AND TOMATO CASSEROLE
A lovely combination of flavours, this dish can be cooked on top of the stove or in the oven.

GRILLED PLAICE FILLETS
The simplest and quickest way of cooking fish. Nothing else is needed with a fresh plaice fillet other than a twist of lemon.

FISH PIE

A childhood favourite that is just as appealing to grown-ups. This dish can be prepared well ahead and cooked as needed.

POACHED SMOKED HADDOCK

Another very easy recipe – with a poached egg popped on top of the fish, this makes an excellent light supper or breakfast.

BAKED SALMON STEAK WITH HERB BUTTER

Just in case you feel like treating yourself – actually this recipe could use *any* fish steak; the delicious butter goes well with all fish.

SOLE GRATIN

A really special dish, in smaller quantities it makes a lovely starter. The recipe can be varied by adding a few prawns. Plaice is good in this dish if preferred.

BAKED TROUT

A whole trout, lightly stuffed then baked, makes a very substantial meal and couldn't be easier to prepare.

COD AND TOMATO CASSEROLE

Serves 1
  1 small onion
  ½ clove garlic
  2 tomatoes
  1 dessertspoon olive oil
  ¼ teaspoon mixed herbs
  1–2 tablespoons white wine
  1 piece of cod fillet
  salt and freshly ground black pepper

To Cook
1) Peel and slice the onion thinly, crush the garlic and peel the tomatoes, discard the seeds and chop the flesh roughly.
2) Heat the oil in a medium-sized pan and cook the onion and garlic until soft but not brown. Add the tomatoes and herbs then pour over the wine.
3) Gently lower in the fish, season lightly then cover and cook over a low heat for about 15 minutes or until the fish is cooked.
   If using an oven, cook at 180°C (350°F) Gas Mark 4, for 20–25 minutes or until the fish is cooked through.

To Serve
Gently lift the fish from the cooking pot, surround with the tomato sauce and serve with plain boiled rice or mashed potatoes.

GRILLED PLAICE FILLETS

Serves 1
  1–2 plaice fillets
  salt and freshly ground black pepper

small knob of butter
freshly chopped parsley
½ lemon

To Cook
1) Pre-heat the grill. Wash the fish and pat dry with
   kitchen paper. Season very lightly with salt and pepper.
   Dot with butter.
2) Cook, right side up, under the grill for 3–5 minutes or
   until the flesh is white and lightly browned on top.

To Serve
Slide the fish on to a warmed plate; sprinkle over a little
freshly chopped parsley and add a twist of lemon.

FISH PIE

Serves 1–2
   400g (1lb) potatoes
   300ml (½pint) milk
   50g (2oz) butter
   200g (8oz) fillet of fish (cod or coley are the most
      suitable)
   salt and freshly ground black pepper
   25g (1oz) flour
   1 teaspoon freshly chopped parsley
   ¼ teaspoon lemon juice

To Cook
1) Pre-heat the oven to 180°C (350°F) Gas Mark 4. Peel
   the potatoes and cook in boiling salted water until soft.
   Drain well, add 1 tablespoon of milk and half the
   butter and mash until light and creamy.
2) Put the fish into a small pan with 2 tablespoons of milk

and season lightly. Bring to the boil, then cover and turn the heat to low; simmer for 5 minutes or so until the fish is cooked.

3) Put the remaining butter, milk and the flour into a small pan, set over medium heat and stir until the ingredients combine and come to the boil. Turn the heat to low and simmer for 2 minutes. Add the parsley and lemon juice.

4) Flake the fish with a fork, discarding any skin or bones.

5) Put the flaked fish into the bottom of an ovenproof dish, pour over the sauce, then gently spoon the potatoes on top.

6) Cook in the oven for 30 minutes or until warmed through and browned on top.

To Serve

Serve straight from the cooking pot, perhaps with grilled tomatoes or peas.

POACHED SMOKED HADDOCK

Serves 1

   1 piece of smoked haddock
   1 tablespoon milk
   15g (½oz) butter
   salt and freshly ground black pepper
   1 egg (optional)

To Cook

1) Put the haddock, milk and butter into a small frying pan. Season lightly. Cover and slowly bring to a simmer.

2) Turn the heat to low and simmer for 3–5 minutes or until the fish is cooked.

To Serve

Lift the fish from the pan gently, drain well. Serve on a warmed plate topped with a poached egg.

BAKED SALMON STEAK WITH HERB BUTTER

Serves 1

    50g (2oz) butter
    1 teaspoon fresh parsley ⎤
    1 teaspoon fresh mint   ⎬ chopped
    ½ teaspoon lemon juice ⎦
    salt and freshly ground black pepper
    1 salmon steak cut 2cm (¾in) thick

To Cook

1) Cream the butter then mix in the herbs and lemon juice, season lightly. Roll into a sausage shape using some greaseproof paper to cover the butter as you roll it. Chill the butter in the fridge for at least 1 hour.
2) Pre-heat the oven to 220°C (425°F) Gas Mark 7. Put a couple of thin slices of the herb butter on top of the salmon steak and wrap it in foil, shiny side inwards.
3) Bake for 12–15 minutes depending on the thickness of the steak.

To Serve

Lift the steak from the foil on to a warmed plate and top with the remaining cold butter cut into two. Discard the foil. (Sometimes the fish is served in the foil it was cooked in, but this does look a mess and you have the foil left on the plate throughout the meal).

Any left-over butter can be kept in a cool place and used to flavour potatoes or grilled meat such as a lamb cutlet or steak.

SOLE GRATIN

Serves 1

  50g (2oz) button mushrooms
  1 spring onion
  25g (1oz) butter
  1 small fillet of sole
  150ml (¼pint) milk
  1 level tablespoon flour
  salt and freshly ground black pepper
  25g (1oz) grated cheese (Gruyère is best but Cheddar
    will do)
  pinch of grated nutmeg

To Cook

1) Wipe and slice the mushrooms and onion.
2) Melt half the butter in a small pan, turn the heat to low and put in the sole. Cover and simmer gently for 3–5 minutes or until the fish is cooked.
3) Drain the fish on kitchen paper. Cut into small pieces, discarding any skin or bones as you do so.
4) Heat the remaining butter and cook the mushrooms and onion over a low heat for 2 minutes. Stir in the flour then slowly add the milk, stirring all the time; season lightly. Simmer this sauce gently for 2 minutes. Stir in the grated cheese.
5) Pre-heat the grill. Put the fish into the bottom of a small oven-proof or gratin dish. Cover with the sauce, sprinkle with nutmeg and grill for 2–3 minutes until well browned and bubbling.

To cook in an oven, set to 200°C (400°F) Gas Mark 6 and bake for 10 minutes until well browned.

To Serve

Serve straight from the grill or oven in the cooking dish. Small quantities look particularly appealing when served in a scallop shell.

BAKED TROUT

Serves 1
  1 small onion
  1 small courgette
  15g (½oz) butter
  salt and freshly ground black pepper
  ½ teaspoon lemon juice
  1 small trout, cleaned well

To Cook

1) Pre-heat the oven to 200°C (400°F) Gas Mark 6. Peel and chop the onion into small dice, wipe and slice the courgette thinly.
2) Heat the butter in a small pan then add the onion and cook until soft but not brown. Add the sliced courgette and continue cooking slowly until soft. Season lightly and sprinkle with lemon juice.
3) Wash and dry the trout inside and out. Put the stuffing into the middle of the fish and secure with a cocktail stick.
4) Bake for 25 minutes or until the fish is cooked through.

To Serve

Put the fish, whole, on to a warmed plate and serve with a twist of lemon.

Vegetables

A carefully cooked vegetable says far more about the cook than practically anything else! The best restaurants hang their reputations on the crunchiness of their veg, and with good reason.

'Don't do it! Relax – simmer gently'

Cooking vegetables properly is a far cry from throwing them into a pan of water, adding salt and boiling like mad! Don't do it! Relax – simmer gently for a shorter period of time and you will find that a tenderly cooked pea really does taste more tender.

Some of the following recipes can be used as starters, main course or side dishes.

The recipes in this section are:

How to cook new potatoes.
How to cook cabbage greens.

NEW POTATO GATEAU
This takes a little time to assemble but once ready for the oven it can be left for a few hours and baked as needed; worth the effort as it really is an impressive dish to serve with any meat or on its own.

DAUPHINOISE POTATOES
This beautifully smooth French classic is very easy to do.

HASH BROWNS
The American 'breakfast' potato dish, also good for lunch, tea, dinner and supper!

GLAZED CARROTS
Simply done, these carrots look and taste wonderful!

BRUSSELS SPROUTS WITH BACON
An interesting combination of texture and flavour, very good with poultry.

CAULIFLOWER POLONAISE
The combination of dry ingredients makes a pleasant change from the more usual cheese sauce.

PEAS WITH SPRING ONIONS
One of the very best ways of cooking fresh peas. You can use the same recipe to cook frozen ones.

RATATOUILLE

The marvellous Mediterranean dish, absolutely delicious, hot or cold.

BAKED RICE

An easy recipe, trouble-free and the finished rice is good, separate and well flavoured.

STUFFED TOMATOES

Lovely as a starter or side dish for grilled meats, this is a recipe that can be varied at will.

HOW TO COOK NEW POTATOES

Serves 1
200–300g (½–¾lb) small new potatoes
1 sprig of fresh mint
salt and freshly ground black pepper
15g (½oz) butter
1 teaspoon freshly chopped parsley

To Cook
1) Scrub the potatoes well, do not peel.
2) Put the clean potatoes and a sprig of mint into a small saucepan. Cover with cold water, season lightly with salt and bring to the boil over medium heat.
3) Turn the heat to low and simmer gently for 10–15 minutes until the potatoes are just cooked. Drain well.
4) Return to the pan, put in the butter, add a few twists of the black pepper and salt mills then shake carefully over medium heat to crisp the skins very slightly.

To Serve
Turn into a warmed dish and sprinkle with a little freshly chopped parsley.

HOW TO COOK CABBAGE GREENS

Serves 1
200g (8oz) cabbage greens
salt and freshly ground black pepper
pinch of bicarbonate of soda
15g (½oz) butter
¼ clove garlic, crushed

To Cook

1) Shred the cabbage finely, discarding any tough veins. Wash well then drain.

2) Bring a pan of lightly salted water to the boil. Add the pinch of bicarb then put in the cabbage. Cover, turn the heat down to low and simmer gently for 2–3 minutes. *No longer.*

3) Drain the cabbage well; melt the butter in the pan, add the garlic and a little black pepper. Return the cabbage to the pan and stir around in the butter for 1 minute.

To Serve

Turn the cabbage into a heated dish and serve at once. Never, ever keep cabbage hot, it takes so little time to cook, it should always be fresh.

NEW POTATO GATEAU

Serves 1–2
300–400g (¾–1lb) medium-sized new potatoes
salt and freshly ground black pepper
15g (½oz) butter
½ tablespoon flour
150ml (¼pint) milk
1 hard-boiled egg
½ teaspoon freshly chopped parsley
½ teaspoon freshly chopped chives
1 tablespoon fresh breadcrumbs

To Cook

1) Scrub the potatoes but do not peel. Put them into a small pan, cover with water and season lightly with salt. Bring to the boil over medium heat; turn the heat to low and simmer until almost cooked through. Drain.

2) Peel the potatoes and cut into small dice about 2cm (¾in) square. Set the oven to 180°C (350°F) Gas Mark 4.

3) Put the butter, flour and milk into a small saucepan. Set over low heat and stir until they combine and come to the boil. Turn down the heat and simmer for 2 minutes. Season lightly with salt and pepper.

4) Chop the egg finely. Lightly grease the base and sides of an oven-proof dish. Put a layer of potatoes into the bottom of the dish, sprinkle some egg on top then mask with some of the sauce. Depending on the shape of your dish, make one or two layers in this way finishing with a sauce layer.

5) Mix the herbs and breadcrumbs together and season lightly, then sprinkle these over the final sauce layer.

6) Bake in the oven for 20–30 minutes until the topping is well browned.

To Serve

Serve straight from the cooking pot; no other garnish is needed. (This is a really elegant side dish but some people have been known to eat it on its own as a main course!)

DAUPHINOISE POTATOES

Serves 1–2
    400g (1lb) potatoes
    25g (1oz) butter
    ½ clove garlic
    150ml (1¼pint) milk (approx)

To Cook

1) Pre-heat the oven to 180°C (350°F) Gas Mark 4.
2) Peel the potatoes and slice them 0.5cm (¼in) thick.
3) Grease the base and sides of a shallow oven-proof dish thickly with half of the butter then rub the cut edge of the garlic all over it.
4) Arrange the slices of potato neatly around the dish in layers. Season well with salt and pepper then pour over the milk, adding more or less to just cover the potatoes. Dot with the remaining butter.
5) Bake in the oven for about 1 hour or until the top is well browned and crisp and the potatoes cooked through.

To Serve

Serve straight from the cooking dish.

To vary the recipe slightly you could add a little grated nutmeg or grated cheese to the potatoes before baking.

HASH BROWNS

Serves 1
  200g (8oz) potatoes
  salt and freshly ground black pepper
  15g (½oz) butter
  1 teaspoon olive oil } *or* bacon fat

To Cook
1) Peel the potatoes, halve and then quarter. Put them into a small pan, cover with water, season lightly and bring to the boil. Turn the heat down to low and simmer until amost cooked through. Drain well and cut into small dice 1cm (⅜in) square.
2) Heat the butter and oil (or bacon fat) in a small frying pan. When foaming add the potato dice, turn the heat down and cook until golden brown on all sides.

To Serve
Drain well on kitchen paper, sprinkle with a little salt and serve at once.

GLAZED CARROTS

Serves 1
  2–3 carrots
  ½ teaspoon sugar
  15g (½oz) butter
  salt and freshly ground black pepper

To Cook
1) Peel or scrape the carrots. Cut into sticks about 0.5cm (¼in) thick by 5cm (2in) long.

2) Put the carrot sticks into a small pan, cover with water, add the sugar and butter and season with salt and pepper.

3) Cover the pan tightly and cook the carrots over medium to low heat until almost tender. Take off the lid and continue cooking until the water has evaporated.

To Serve

Sprinkle with a little freshly chopped mint and serve at once.

BRUSSELS SPROUTS WITH BACON

Serves 1

150g (6oz) brussels sprouts
1 rasher smoked bacon
1 teaspoon salted peanuts (optional)
1 small knob of butter
salt and freshly ground black pepper

To Cook

1) Trim the sprouts of any yellowing leaves and woody bits of stalk.

2) Bring a small pan of lightly salted water to the boil, drop in the sprouts, turn the heat down and simmer for 5–7 minutes until almost tender – but still firm. Drain well.

3) While the sprouts are cooking de-rind and grill the bacon until crisp and brown. Cut into small pieces.

4) Melt a small knob of butter in a pan; when foaming add the drained sprouts, nuts (if using) and bacon. Season lightly and toss gently together until well mixed.

To Serve

Turn into a warmed dish and serve.

Chestnuts can be used instead of the peanuts and this is especially good with a traditional Christmas lunch.

CAULIFLOWER POLONAISE

Serves 1–2

  1 small cauliflower
  1 small onion
  15g (½oz) butter
  1 hard-boiled egg
  1 tablespoon fresh breadcrumbs
  25g (1oz) grated cheese (Cheddar for preference)
  ½ teaspoon chopped parsley
  salt and freshly ground black pepper

To Cook

1) Trim the cauliflower and break into florets, leaving a few of the green leaves on if possible.
2) Bring a saucepan of lightly salted water to the boil, drop in the cauliflower, turn down the heat and simmer for about 5 minutes until barely cooked through. Drain well.
3) While the cauliflower cooks prepare the topping. Peel and chop the onion finely. Melt the butter in a small pan; when foaming add the onion and cook until soft but not brown. Remove the pan from the heat.
4) Chop the egg finely and stir into the onion. Add the breadcrumbs, cheese and parsley; season lightly then mix well.
5) Pre-heat the grill. Put the drained cauliflower into an oven-proof dish and cover with the cheese and

breadcrumb mixture. Place the dish under the grill for 2–3 minutes until the cheese melts and the breadcrumbs are well browned.

To Serve
Serve straight from the cooking pot.

This topping also goes well on celery, leeks and fennel; simply adjust the simmering time for each vegetable.

PEAS WITH SPRING ONIONS

Serves 1
  400g (1lb) young green peas in their shells
  2–3 lettuce leaves
  4 spring onions
  salt
  ½ teaspoon sugar
  1 sprig of mint
  15g (½oz) butter

To Cook
1) Shell the peas. Shred the lettuce finely. Cut the spring onions into 5cm (2in) lengths.
2) Put the vegetables into a small pan with just enough cold water to cover. Add the salt, sugar, mint and butter and cover tightly with foil then put the lid on top.
3) Cook steadily over medium to low heat for about 30 minutes, adding a little more water if necessary.

To Serve
Usually the water has evaporated by the time the peas are cooked; if not drain them well and turn the peas into a warmed dish.

RATATOUILLE

Serves 1–2
  200g (8oz) tomatoes
  150g (6oz) aubergine
  100g (4oz) courgette
  50g (2oz) green pepper
  50g (2oz) onion
  ½ small clove garlic
  1 teaspoon freshly chopped basil *or*
  ¼ teaspoon dried basil
  salt and freshly ground black pepper
  1 tablespoon olive oil

To Cook
1) Peel the tomatoes, discard the seeds and chop the flesh roughly. Peel and cut the aubergine into slices 2cm (¾in) thick. Trim and cut the courgette into slices 0.5cm (¼in) thick. After de-seeding, chop the pepper roughly. Peel and slice the onion. Crush the garlic.
2) Put the aubergine and courgette slices on to a plate, sprinkle with salt and leave for 20 minutes to draw out the bitter juices. Rinse and pat dry with kitchen paper.
3) Heat the oil in a medium-sized pan and cook the onion, peppers and garlic for a few minutes until soft but not browned.
4) Put all the other ingredients into the pan. Mix carefully then cover tightly and cook over very low heat for 25–30 minutes until just cooked through.

To Serve
Turn the ratatouille into a warmed dish, sprinkle with a little freshly chopped parsley and serve hot or cold.

BAKED RICE

Serves 1
  1 shallot
  15g (½oz) butter
  50g (2oz) long grain rice
  200ml (⅝pint) chicken stock (made from a stock cube)
  salt and freshly ground black pepper

To Cook

1) Pre-heat the oven to 190°C (375°F) Gas Mark 5. Peel and chop the shallot finely. Melt the butter in a small pan and cook the shallot for 1 minute until soft.
2) Add the rice to the pan and stir thoroughly to coat with the butter. Pour over the stock and bring the mixture to the boil. Season lightly.
3) Turn the rice into an oven-proof dish, cover and cook in the oven for about 25 minutes or until the stock is absorbed and the rice is tender.

To Serve

Turn the rice on to a warmed plate and fluff up the grains with a fork so that they are separate.

STUFFED TOMATOES

Serves 1
  1–2 good-sized tomatoes
  ½ rasher bacon
  ½ small onion
  1 tablespoon fresh breadcrumbs
  ½ teaspoon freshly chopped parsley
  1 teaspoon grated cheese
  salt and freshly ground black pepper

To Cook

1) Pre-heat the oven to 180°C (350°F) Gas Mark 4. Slice the top(s) off the tomato(es), scoop out the seeds and pulp with a small spoon. Discard the seeds. Turn the tomato shell(s) upside down to drain. Chop the pulp roughly.
2) Derind the bacon and cut into small pieces. Peel and chop the onion.
3) Cook the bacon in its own fat until lightly browned, add the onion and cook for 2–3 minutes until soft. Remove the pan from the heat and stir in the bread-crumbs, parsley, tomato pulp and cheese. Season lightly.
4) Spoon the stuffing into the tomato case(s). Put the slice(s) from the top(s) back on as a lid. Place the tomato(es) in an oven-proof dish and bake for 20 minutes.

To Serve

Using a fish slice or palette knife, slide the tomato(es) on to a warmed plate and serve at once. (Avoid using tongs to transfer the tomato(es); they are soft in the middle when cooked and the filling squashes out with a 'plop'. Not recommended!)

Salads

There are good salads that are a delicious mix of basically raw ingredients held together with a light and complementary dressing, and then there is the other sort of salad: limp lettuce leaves, a quarter of tomato and a soggy slice of cucumber, usually with a black speck somewhere amongst them. This chapter deals with the former!

The ideas in this section of the book are really quite basic and are intended to be used as a guide to assembling salads and dressings to your own tastes. There are recipes for four dressings each with its own distinct character. They are:

LIGHT VINAIGRETTE
The simplest dressing of all made from olive oil and vinegar and seasoning.

VINAIGRETTE
The 'beefier' version of the above dressing uses herbs, onions, garlic and mustard to give it more body and bite.

MAYONNAISE
Always useful to have 'in'. This recipe will store for up to 1 week in the fridge.

CREAMY HERB DRESSING
A really delicious dressing, especially good on a cooked vegetable salad.

The basic salad recipes are:

GREEN SALAD
Just that.

TOMATO SALAD
Excellent with grills and barbecues.

MIXED VEGETABLE SALAD
Using a combination of cooked or raw vegetables. •

SALAD NIÇOISE
Another classic for which everyone has their own favourite recipe. This recipe is the most basic.

SALAD COMPOSÉE
With ham and cheese, a good salad for a first course or as a light meal.

SAUSAGE, BEAN AND APPLE SALAD
A substantial dish most suitable for a light meal.

COLESLAW
Much crunchier than the ready-made stuff.

LIGHT VINAIGRETTE

1 teaspoon wine vinegar *or* lemon juice
salt and freshly ground black pepper
1–2 teaspoons olive oil

To Make
1) Put the vinegar into a small bowl, season lightly with salt and pepper, and beat with a fork until dissolved.
2) Add the oil drop by drop, beating all the time until the dressing is well blended and cloudy. Use at once.

VINAIGRETTE

½ teaspoon lemon juice
1 tablespoon olive oil
1 teaspoon wine vinegar
pinch of salt
¼ teaspoon sugar
¼ teaspoon French mustard
pinch dry mustard
¼ clove garlic, crushed
1 spring onion, finely chopped
¼ teaspoon mixed herbs

To Make
1) Put all the ingredients into a small container with a tight-fitting lid. Shake well and use at once.

MAYONNAISE

1 egg yolk
½ level teaspoon salt

½ level teaspoon dry mustard
¼ level teaspoon white pepper
½ level teaspoon sugar
150ml (¼pint) olive oil
2 teaspoons white wine vinegar, *or* lemon juice
1 teaspoon boiling water

To Make
1) Put the egg yolk into a basin and stir in the salt, mustard, pepper and sugar.
2) When thoroughly blended add one drop of olive oil, beat briskly with a wooden spoon then add one more drop of oil. Beat well again and continue adding the oil drop by drop and beating until the mayonnaise is thick and smooth.
3) Beat in the vinegar (or lemon juice) and hot water. In the unlikely event of the mayonnaise curdling, beat in another egg yolk.

CREAMY HERB DRESSING

1 teaspoon white wine vinegar
salt and freshly ground black pepper
1 tablespoon olive oil
1 tablespoon double cream
1 teaspoon parsley
1 teaspoon chives   freshly chopped
1 teaspoon tarragon

To Make
1) Put the wine vinegar into a bowl and add some salt and pepper. Stir until dissolved.
2) Beat in the olive oil drop by drop then add the cream. Beat again and when well blended add the herbs. Use at once.

GREEN SALAD

Serves 1–2
    3–4 crisp lettuce leaves
    2–3 sprigs watercress
    1 small green pepper
    ¼ small cucumber
    2–3 spring onions
    1 tablespoon light vinaigrette dressing

To Make
1) Wash the lettuce and watercress and dry well on kitchen paper.
2) De-seed and slice the pepper into thin rings. Wipe and slice the cucumber thinly. Trim and chop the onions.
3) Put the vegetables into a bowl, pour over the dressing and mix well.

To Serve
Serve at once.

TOMATO SALAD

Serves 1
    2–3 tomatoes
    1 tablespoon vinaigrette dressing
    1–2 spring onions, finely chopped

To Make
1) Slice the tomatoes 0.5cm (¼in) thick, and arrange in a shallow dish. Pour over the vinaigrette. Chill for 30 minutes in the fridge. Sprinkle the spring onions on top.

To Serve
Gently turn the tomatoes over once with a fish slice or
pallet knife and serve from the shallow dish.

MIXED VEGETABLE SALAD

Serves 1
   1–2 medium-sized new potatoes, cooked
   1 courgette
   2–3 spring onions
   2–3 crisp lettuce leaves
   1–2 tablespoons creamy herb dressing

To Make
1) Dice the potatoes into 2cm (¾in) squares.
2) Cut the courgette into slices 0.5cm (¼in) thick. Slice
   the onions into 4cm (1½in) lengths.
3) Bring a pan of lightly salted water to the boil and cook
   the courgette and spring onion for 1 minute, then drain
   well.
4) Line a bowl with the lettuce leaves. Put in the other
   vegetables, pour over the dressing and chill for 30
   minutes.

To Serve
Gently turn the vegetables over in the dressing and serve
at once.

SALAD NIÇOISE

Serves 2
   2–3 crisp lettuce leaves
   4–6 French beans, cooked

1 small onion
½ small green pepper
½ small red pepper
2 tomatoes
1 anchovy fillet
1 small tin tuna
6–8 slices of cucumber
6–8 black olives
2 tablespoons vinaigrette dressing
1 hard-boiled egg

To Make

1) Wash and dry the lettuce leaves. Cut up the beans, peel and chop the onion, de-seed and chop the peppers. Quarter the tomatoes, chop the anchovy very thinly, drain and flake the tuna.
2) Use the lettuce to line a bowl, arrange all the ingredients on top of it with the exception of the egg.
3) Pour over the vinaigrette, turn the salad over a few times. Chill for 20 minutes.

To Serve

Peel and quarter the egg and arrange the sections on the salad.

SALAD COMPOSÉE

Serves 1–2
2–3 crisp lettuce leaves
25g (1oz) Cheddar cheese
25g (1oz) boiled ham
1–2 small potatoes, cooked
1 tomato
1 tablespoon creamy herb dressing *or* mayonnaise

To Make
1) Wash and dry the lettuce and use to line a bowl.
2) Cut the cheese into small dice 0.5cm (¼in) square. Cut the ham and potatoes into small pieces. Quarter the tomato. Pile these ingredients on top of the lettuce and pour over the dressing. Stir gently.
3) Chill for 10 minutes.

To Serve
Turn the vegetables and cheese over gently with a spoon and serve from the bowl.

SAUSAGE, BEAN AND APPLE SALAD

Serves 1–2
    1–2 potatoes, cooked
    2 pork sausages, cooked
    1 hard green eating apple
    1 spring onion
    1 small can cooked red kidney beans
    1 tomato
    good pinch of paprika
    1–2 tablespoons vinaigrette dressing

To Make
1) Cut the potato(es), sausage and apple into evenly sized pieces. Chop the spring onion finely. Drain the beans. Quarter the tomato.
2) Combine these ingredients together in a bowl, season with paprika and pour over the dressing. Mix and chill for 30 minutes.

To Serve
Stir the salad gently and serve straight from the bowl.

COLESLAW

Serves 1–2
  ¼ small white cabbage
  1 small carrot
  ½ small onion
  1 tablespoon mayonnaise *or* creamy herb dressing

To Make
1) Shred the cabbage as thinly as possible.
2) Peel and grate the carrot and onion.
3) Mix the three vegetables together with the dressing and chill for 15 minutes.

To Serve
Stir once or twice to mix and serve straight from the chilled dish.

Grated onion is very strongly flavoured; finely chopped or sliced onion may be substituted if preferred.

Sweets

As everyone knows, it is better to finish off a meal with a piece of fresh fruit than a stodgy pud! But . . .

When boredom sets in or for a special dinner, try one of the following dishes; they are all easy to prepare, delicious *and* fattening!

The recipes are:

FRESH FRUIT SALAD
Lots of scope for experimenting here; just make the syrup and add your favourite fruits.

OLD ENGLISH TRIFLE
Another great favourite, this recipe is a traditional one and doesn't use jelly.

MILLE FEUILLES
Using ready-made puff pastry – this is almost too easy. Good though and quite impressive.

GOOSEBERRY CRUMBLE
This recipe can be used for any fruit crumble.

BAKED CUSTARD
A good stand-by, this dish can be cooked whenever you have the oven on for something else.

PASTEL DE MANZANA
Known as 'toe-nails' in certain quarters. It is a delicious combination of apples, cinnamon and mint with a crunchy topping.

CHOCOLATE PEARS

Lightly poached pears covered in a beautiful chocolate sauce.

BAKED APPLE

A very easy pudding and a great favourite. Try experimenting with different fillings.

NO-BAKE CHOCOLATE CAKE

A most useful recipe, it keeps well and is handy to have 'in'. It is an excellent alternative to 'after-dinner mints' and boxed attractively makes a very special gift. Keep cool at all times though, or the chocolate melts!

FRESH FRUIT SALAD

Serves 1–2
  100g (4oz) caster sugar
  150ml (¼pint) water
  1 teaspoon lemon juice
  1 apple
  1 pear
  1 clementine
  4–6 grapes
  1 small wedge of melon

To Make

1) Put the sugar and water into a small pan. Stir over a low heat until the sugar dissolves then simmer for 2 minutes. Add the lemon juice. Allow to cool then pour into a glass serving dish.
2) Peel and core the apple and pear and cut into small chunks. Put into the syrup. Peel and segment the clementine, removing any bits of pith and any pips. Halve the grapes and flick out any pips. Peel and cut the melon into chunks. Add each fruit to the dish as it is prepared. Stir well then chill for 1 hour.

To Serve

Take the bowl from the fridge just before the fruit salad is needed. If you wish to include banana, add this at the very last moment since it quickly turns brown and soggy.

Other combinations can be made interesting by restricting the fruits to certain colours. Green is easy in winter with kiwi fruit, grapes, melon and Granny Smith apples. Orange is a lovely summer colour, with peaches, apricots, nectarines.

OLD ENGLISH TRIFLE

Serves 1–2
   1 small plain sponge cake
   1 tablespoon raspberry jam
   2–3 macaroon biscuits *or* ratafias
   1–2 tablespoons sherry
   1 teaspoon sugar
   1 egg yolk
   100ml (1/6 pint) milk
   2–3 tablespoons double cream

To Make
1) Split the sponge cake and spread with the jam. Put into the bottom of a glass serving dish. Put in the macaroons and sprinkle with the sherry.
2) Whisk the sugar and egg yolk together in a small bowl until light and creamy. Warm the milk but do not allow to boil.
3) Pour the warmed milk on to the egg mixture and return to the pan.
4) Cook over a low heat, whisking all the time until the custard thickens enough to coat the back of a spoon.
5) Pour over the cake and biscuits whilst still warm. Chill well.

To Serve
Whip the double cream until it thickens and spoon on top of the trifle. Decorate, if liked, with crystallized fruits or glacé cherries.

MILLE FEUILLES

Serves 2–3
   200g (7oz) puff pastry (frozen is most suitable de-
      frosted)
   2 tablespoons jam
   150ml (¼pint) double cream
   4 tablespoons icing sugar
   2–3 drops lemon juice

To Cook
1) Pre-heat the oven to 180°C (350°F) Gas Mark 6. Divide
   the pastry into two and roll out on a lightly floured
   board into rectangles measuring 15 × 8cm (6 × 3in).
2) Put on to a greased baking tray and cook for 10–12
   minutes until puffed-up and golden brown. Cool on a
   wire rack (from the bottom of the grill pan perhaps).
3) Mix the icing sugar with a little water and lemon juice,
   adding it drop by drop until you have a stiffish paste,
   glossy and with no lumps.
4) Spread the icing over the flat side of one piece of cooled
   pastry using the back of a spoon or a pallet knife.
   Leave a 1cm (⅜in) margin all round so that the icing
   doesn't creep away over the edge.
5) Spread the jam on to the puffy side of the other piece
   of pastry. Whip the cream until stiff and spoon it on
   top of the jam. Put the iced pastry on top – icing side
   up.

To Serve
Not the easiest sweet to handle when it comes to slicing.
Try starting from the middle using a sharp serrated edge
knife and a little pressure.

GOOSEBERRY CRUMBLE

Serves 2

> 200g (8oz) gooseberries
> 75g (3oz) sugar (more or less, depending on the
>   sweetness of the fruit)
> 75g (3oz) flour
> pinch of salt
> scant 40g (1½oz) butter

To Cook

1) Pre-heat the oven to 200°C (400°F) Gas Mark 6. Top and tail the gooseberries, leave whole and place into the bottom of a small oven-proof dish. Sprinkle with 50g (2oz) sugar and 1 tablespoon of water.
2) Sift the flour and salt into a bowl, add the butter and work it into the flour with your finger-tips until absorbed and the mixture looks like breadcrumbs.
3) Mix the remaining sugar into the flour mixture and tip evenly over the fruit. Bake for 30–40 minutes, until the fruit is cooked and the crumble lightly browned.

To Serve

Serve hot or cold with custard, either the baked or the pouring sort. (The recipe for pouring custard is given in the trifle instructions. You didn't really think you would get away with the packet sort, did you!)

BAKED CUSTARD

Serves 1–2

> 150ml (¼pint) milk
> 1 large egg
> 1 teaspoon caster sugar
> 1 drop vanilla essence (optional)

To Cook

1) Pre-heat the oven to 180°C (350°F) Gas Mark 4. Heat the milk (with the vanilla essence if using) in a small pan; do not allow to boil.
2) Whisk the egg and sugar together until fluffy. Pour over the milk and strain into a small oven-proof dish.
3) Pour some cold water into a large oven-proof dish (not metal) and stand the custard dish in this to cook.
4) Put on to a low shelf in the oven and bake for 1¼–1½ hours or until set.

To Serve

The custard can be served hot or cold.

PASTEL DE MANZANA

Serves 2–3

   400g (1lb) cooking apples
   1 level teaspoon cinnamon
   1 level teaspoon dried mint
   15g (½oz) butter (for greasing the baking dish)
   75g (3oz) flour
   pinch of salt
   100g (4oz) sugar
   1 small egg, beaten
   ½ teaspoon baking powder

To Cook

1) Pre-heat the oven to 180°C (350°F) Gas Mark 4. Peel and core the apples and slice thinly. Put into a bowl. Sprinkle over the cinnamon and mint and toss the apple slices until well coated.
2) Butter a shallow oven-proof dish thickly, put the apples into the bottom of it.

3) Sift together the flour, salt, and baking powder.
4) Mix in the sugar, then pour in the egg. 'Cut' the egg into the mixture with a knife until absorbed. Tip the topping over the apples and press down lightly.
5) Bake for 40 minutes, when the apple should be cooked and the topping light brown and crisp.

To Serve

Serve hot with custard or cold with ice cream. This is a very distinctive sweet and although a little unusual it really is delicious.

CHOCOLATE PEARS

Serves 1–2
  1–2 good-sized pears
  ½ lemon
  25g (1oz) sugar
  150ml (¼pint) water
  50g (2oz) dark chocolate

To Cook

1) Peel the pears but leave the stalks intact. Rub over with the cut side of the lemon.
2) Dissolve the sugar in the water in a small pan over low heat. Gently lower in the pears and simmer, covered, for 20 minutes until cooked but firm.
3) Lift the pears from the pan, using the stalks to do so, and stand each on a small plate. Chill.
4) Boil the syrup rapidly until reduced to 1 tablespoon. Break the chocolate into small pieces and stir into the hot syrup.

To Serve
Spoon the sauce over the pears. Serve with the sauce warm or cold.

BAKED APPLE

Serves 1
>   1 large Bramley apple
>   1 teaspoon raisins
>   1 teaspoon chopped walnuts
>   2 teaspoons honey

To Cook
1) Pre-heat the oven to 180°C (350°F) Gas Mark 4. Wipe and core the apple leaving it whole; make a small cut into the skin all the way around the middle.
2) Combine the raisins, nuts and honey and push the resulting mixture into the centre of the apple.
3) Put the apple on a small oven-proof dish and bake for 15–20 minutes or until soft.

To Serve
Serve hot with custard.

NO-BAKE CHOCOLATE CAKE

Makes one 18cm (7in) cake
>   50g (2oz) butter
>   150g (6oz) dark chocolate
>   200g (8oz) rich tea biscuits
>   25g (1oz) glacé cherries
>   1 egg, beaten
>   25g (1oz) raisins
>   6 walnut halves

To Cook

1) Melt the butter and chocolate in a small pan, stirring together over low heat. Break up the biscuits. Chop the cherries into four pieces.
2) When the butter chocolate mixture is smooth, add the egg, biscuits, cherries and raisins and stir well until combined.
3) Line a 18cm (7in) cake tin with silicone paper. Press the mixture well down into the tin. Chill for 2–3 hours until set.

To Serve

Turn out of the tin, invert and decorate with the walnuts. Serve cut into wedges.

In an airtight container, this cake will keep (in a cool place) for a week. To serve as an after-dinner chocolate, press into a square or oblong container and leave to set. Cut into 2.5cm (1in) cubes and decorate with pieces of walnut and cherries.

Snacks

Although the idea of this book is to show that eating sensibly and well is possible even in the most unusual circumstances, snacks do have their place. The following are all quickly prepared and very tasty.

TOASTED SANDWICHES
Any type of grill will do to make these. If you have no grill at all just follow the recipe for Croque Monsieur (page 125), varying the fillings as you wish.

'Any type of grill will do to make these'

It is best to butter the bread first, on the outside of the sandwich. Use a fairly hard cheese such as Cheddar, Double Gloucester or Leicester. Cheshire and Lancashire are best for cheese on toast but seem a little strong for a sandwich. Edam and Gruyère tend to go rather stringy which can be fun but does not make for elegant eating!

SUGGESTED FILLINGS
CHEESE AND THINLY SLICED ONION OR
   TOMATO
CHEESE AND A SLICE OF BOILED HAM WITH
   THINLY SLICED APPLE
CHEESE AND A SPRINKLING OF PRAWNS OR
   SHRIMPS
CHEESE AND VERY FINELY CHOPPED HERBS
   WITH A LITTLE GRATED ONION
SARDINE AND SLICED TOMATO
TUNA AND CHOPPED EGG
COOKED SMOKED BACON AND CHEESE.

CROQUE MONSIEUR

Serves 1
   2 slices bread cut 0.5cm (½in) thick
   1 slice cooked ham (lean)
   25g (1oz) Gruyère cheese, thinly sliced
   Sewing thread
   15g (½oz) butter

To Make

1) Cover one slice of bread firstly with ham then with cheese. Top with the remaining slice of bread and tie into a parcel with the cotton.
2) Melt the butter in a frying pan. Sauté the parcel on each side until golden brown.
3) Snip off the cotton and serve at once.

NB To make a Croque Madame, serve topped with a fried egg.

SANDWICHES

When time is especially important don't under-estimate the value of a good sandwich. They can be prepared and wrapped in clingfilm to keep fresh until needed. If you experiment with interesting fillings and substitute cream cheese or mayonnaise for butter from time to time, the possibilities are endless. And why not try all the different sorts of bread that are available nowadays.

Here are just a few ideas to get you going:

COLD GRILLED STREAKY BACON, sliced tomato and lettuce on wholegrain bread spread with mayonnaise.

COTTAGE CHEESE AND A LITTLE FINELY CHOPPED ONION sprinkled with curry powder on hollowed-out crusty French bread.

PILCHARDS IN TOMATO SAUCE mashed with thinly sliced cucumber sprinkled with vinegar on malted wholegrain bread.

CHILLED SLICED RADISHES on brown bread thickly spread with cream cheese.

CORNED BEEF AND LETTUCE on sesame seed bread spread *lightly* with creamed horse radish one side, English mustard on the other. (Known as 'The Killer' – it's really good though!)

HARD BOILED EGG (see method on page 36 to make sure you don't get a black ring around the yolk) mashed with butter, salt, finely chopped green or red pepper and onion on wholemeal bread.

'Don't under-estimate the value of a good sandwich'

Index